AF840646

Amtrak Police

Christian Berna

2025

Amtrak Police

Christian Berna

Copyright ©2025 by **Christian Berna and Eric Thomsen**

All rights reserved. Without limiting the rights under copyright reserved above, no part of this publication may be reproduced, stored in or introduced into a retrieval system, or transmitted, in any form, or by any means (electronic, mechanical, photocopying, recording or otherwise) without the prior written permission of both the copyright owner and the above publisher of this book.

The pictures of the prints are in the public domain in its country of origin and other countries and areas where the copyright term is the author's life plus 100 years or less, or because a licence has been granted. This book is void of sale where disallowed.

US ISBN 978-9-7132-4635-6

This book is available in color print in the United States under ISBN 978-4-753-507-726

Introduction

The Amtrak Police Department (APD) is a federal law enforcement agency that provides security and law enforcement services for Amtrak, the national passenger train system in the United States.

The Amtrak Police Department is responsible for the safety and security of Amtrak passengers, employees, and infrastructure across the country. The APD has primary jurisdiction over Amtrak stations, trains, rights-of-way, and maintenance facilities. They also have jurisdiction over crimes committed against Amtrak, its employees, or its passengers. APD officers patrol stations, trains, and facilities, enforce laws, conduct investigations, and provide support at events. They also work with other agencies, such as local law enforcement, and participate in joint operations and training exercises.

The APD has over 500 sworn and civilian personnel at over 30 locations across 46 states, the District of Columbia, and three Canadian provinces. The APD has specialized units like the Special Operations Unit, which conducts station surges, baggage screening, and counter-surveillance operations. They also have a robust K-9 program and a National Communications Center for dispatch and incident response. The APD collaborates with other law enforcement agencies, emergency responders, and other Amtrak stakeholders through programs like Operation RAILSAFE to enhance safety and security. This book was finished on July 4, 2025 and I hope that you enjoy my selection of pictures. Happy 4th of July!

Christian

No 1 Amtrak Police Officer in golf cart in front of Union Station at 50 Massachusetts Avenue, NE, Washington DC on Thursday morning, 19 March 2020.

The Amtrak Police Department (APD) is the national police force responsible for the safety and security of Amtrak's customers, employees, and infrastructure.

No 2 Amtrak Police Officer at the Information Desk at Penn Station at 1500 North Charles Street in Baltimore, Maryland on Tuesday night, 25 February 2020 by Elvert Barnes Photography.

Amtrak police operate in 46 states, the District of Columbia, and three Canadian provinces.

No 3 Protecting America's railroads, September 15, 2012. This is a K9 Chevrolet Tahoe in front of Washington D.C. station. It is parked in Union Station Plaza or Columbus Plaza.

The pigeons are not scared.

No 4 An Amtrak Police SUV at the Lancaster Amtrak station in Lancaster, Pennsylvania, October 6, 2010.

This is a Ford Expedition K9. The Ford Expedition K9 is a specialized version of the Ford Expedition SUV designed for police and law enforcement use, particularly for transporting and housing police dogs (K9 units).

No 5 Amtrak Police Ford Expedition SUVs parked on 8th Avenue south of 33rd Street in front of Penn Station and Madison Square Garden in Midtown Manhattan. November 20, 2017.

These are not standard trim level vehceles, but special configurations built by third-party companies.

No 6 Amtrak Police K9 Unit at Union Station Train Concourse at 50 Massachusetts Avenue, NE, Washington DC on Friday morning, 31 January 2020 by Elvert Barnes Photography.

The Amtrak Police Departament has over 500 sworn and civilian personnel who conduct security measures both behind the scenes and on the front lines.

No 7 A front view of Union Station, Portland, Oregon. The Portland Union Station opened in 1896 after several delays. It was one part of Henry Villard's grand vision for Portland. Villard wanted to make Portland an important city.

No 8 Two Amtrak Police Ford Expedition K9 SUVs in front of the Washington D.C. station, July 22, 2011.

The Amtrak Police use the Ford Expedition because it is a reliable and versatile vehicle that can handle the demands of police work in various environments, including urban areas and along the railroad right-of-way.

Amtrak only owns 623 miles of track, the vast majority of the routes it uses are owned by private freight railroads.

No 9 Amtrak Police June 7, 2016. The Ford Expedition SUV offers a spacious interior for transporting equipment and personnel, as well as a powerful engine and robust suspension for navigating diverse terrains.

Diverse terrain you will find along the right of way of the railroad.

Amtrak operates on a network of over 21,400 route miles, but it owns only a small fraction of this track, approximately 623 miles, and Amtrak pays for access rights to run its passenger trains on those other lines.

No 10 1st Annual Police K-9 Memorial Service Ceremony at the National Law Enforcement Officers Memorial Central Plaza at Judiciary Square, NW, Washington DC on Friday afternoon, 11 May 2018 by Elvert Barnes Photography. The Annual Police K-9 Memorial Service Ceremony honors the lives and service of police dogs who have died in the line of duty. It's part of National Police Week in Washington, D.C., and includes a wreath and rose laying ceremony. The event, hosted by the National Police Dog Foundation, also recognizes the handlers and departments that lost their K-9 partners.

No 11 Amtrak Police Ford Expedition SUV from the Washington, D.C. Station July 22, 2011.

This is a great picture, it has good lighting, a dynamic angle and the setting complements the Police car’s use. When you set out to take a great photograph, it is important to consider three key elements: the subject, the background, and the light. Great photographs often include an engaging subject set in a neutral or complementary background, bathed in soft light

No 12 Amtrak Police Ford Expedition SUV K9 in front of the Washington D.C. station, July 22, 2011.

This is a special configuration built by third-party companies like Havis or American Aluminum, who offer K9 transport systems for various vehicles.

Havis, Inc. is an American company that manufactures in-vehicle mobile office and prisoner transport products for public safety, government, and enterprise fleet.s

No 13 Amtrak police, August 21, 2011. Two Ford Expedition SUVs in what appears to be Milwaukee, Wisconsin because of the flag which is rectangular and the colors of the flag yellow, blue, and brown.

Milwaukee Intermodal Station is an intercity bus and train station in downtown Milwaukee, Wisconsin. Amtrak service at Milwaukee includes the daily Empire Builder, the daily Borealis, and the six daily Hiawatha round trips

No 14 Amtrak Police Officer at Union Station at 50 Massachusetts Avenue, NE, Washington DC on Saturday afternoon, 14 November 2020 by Elvert Barnes Photography.

There is some extra action in this photo.

No 15 Amtrak Police Chevrolet Tahoe K9 SUV. The Amtrak Police Department is a railroad police agency whose aim is to act as the law enforcement arm of the (partially) government funded American national rail service, Amtrak. Its approximately 500 officers (most of whom are stationed in the Northeast Corridor, where Amtrak is busiest) guard Amtrak stations, maintenance facilities, and trains. They've become much more focused on counter-terror activity since 9/11. October 10, 2014.

No 16 Amtrak police officer watches a special train at Burlington station in April 2015.

Railroad police officers serving in the Eastern corridor were commonly called "detectives." In the west, they earned the name "Special Agents." This title persevered throughout the years. Two of the most famous Special Agents hired to protect the railroads were Bat Masterson and Allen Pinkerton.

No 17 Amtrak Police Dodge Durango SUV K9, August 17, 2011.

These Durangos are equipped with K-9 transport systems and are often seen as part of the APD's fleet of patrol vehicles. The Amtrak Police Department utilizes K-9 units for various tasks, including explosives and narcotics detection, and vapor wake detection.

No 18 Amtrak Police Officers at Union Station at 50 Massachusetts Avenue, NE, Washington DC on Saturday afternoon, 14 November 2020 by Elvert Barnes Photograpy.

Amtrak Police Officers regularly patrol stations, trains, and surrounding areas to prevent crime and ensure passenger safety. They enforce both federal and local laws within Amtrak's jurisdiction. Their presence acts as a deterrent to potential criminal activity.

No 19 Amtrak Police Ford Expedition SUV K9, August 17, 2011.

K9 systems, often fabricated from heavy-duty aluminum, are designed to securely and comfortably transport the dogs, maximizing space for the driver and the dog. While some Amtrak K-9 units may be fully marked, others are semi-marked, meaning they have minimal exterior markings to potentially blend in while still being recognizable as a police vehicle.

American Aluminum makes "K-9" units, which are specialized vehicle inserts for transporting police and military dogs.

No 20 Amtrak Police Ford Expedition SUV at Union Station, November 7th, 2011.

On November 7th, 2011, the main event at Union Station, specifically in New York City, was the arrest of a suspected groper who allegedly assaulted a co-ed in a Union Square subway station.

No 21 Amtrak Police Ford Expedition SUV K9, August 17, 2011. It is an interesting image because the lights are mirrored in the windows. It looks like New York. Amtrak K9 units are primarily used to enhance safety and security on trains and in stations by detecting explosives and narcotics, and also serve as a deterrent to crime. Amtrak has more than 50 police dogs, and some are equipped with vapor wake capabilities. They work with their human partners to protect passengers and employees from various threats.

No 22 Amtrak Police Officer at Union Station Lower Level in NE Washington DC on Saturday morning, 21 January 2017 by Elvert Barnes Photography.

There are many people using Amtrak and some of them are not respecting the rules and it is nececary for the Amtrak police officers to look tough.

No 23 Amtrak Police Department, August 17, 2011. This picture is taken at Penn station, Midtown West, Manhattan. It's a Ford Expedition K9 SUV. Penn Station, officially Pennsylvania Station, is a major transportation hub located in Midtown Manhattan, which is the busiest transportation facility in the Western Hemisphere. Approximately 600,000 people use New York's Penn Station daily. The station serves as a hub for Amtrak, Long Island Rail Road, New Jersey Transit, and the New York City subway.

No 24 An Amtrak Police Ford Expedition SUV at the Lancaster Amtrak station in Lancaster, Pennsylvania. October 6, 2010. This station is the gateway to the Aimish Country.

The Amish people are members of a conservative Protestant Christian group known for their plain dress, simple living, and rejection of many modern conveniences. Amish communities live, most notably Lancaster County, Pennsylvania but laso I Ohio and Indiana.

No 25 Amtrak Police Department Ford Transit Prisoner transport van, August 17, 2011. This picture is taken at Penn Station, Midtown West, Manhattan.

With more than 600.000 passengers using the station every day sometimes you need to remove some of them. Penn Station, as a major transportation hub, sees a variety of criminal activity, with petty theft, public lewdness, and homelessness being the most prevalent issues.

No 26 Amtrak Police patrol Hiawatha two days before 2024 RNC, July 13, 2024. The 2024 RNC convention was the first normal in-person presidential nominating convention since virtual 2020.

No 27 Amtrak Police Department Dodge Durango K9 SUV, August 17, 2011.

While overall felony crime has been trending downward in the Midtown South Precinct which includes Penn Station, there have been upticks in murder, rape, and felony assault this last year. That's why its nececary to have Amtrak Police around.

No 28 The Stockton – San Joaquin Street Station in Stockton, California, USA., October 13, 2012.

The cae is a Dodge Charger. The Dodge Charger Pursuit is a popular police vehicle due to its powerful engine options. The Charger Pursuit is designed with police-specific features like ballistic door panels, steel seatbacks, and a trunk ventilation system.

No 29 Amtrak Police Department Ford Expedition K9 SUV, outside Penn station, Midtown West, Manhattan. August 17, 2011. Penn Station is famous for its history as a grand architectural landmark and a major transportation hub.

No 30 Amtrak Police patrol the Hiawatha two days before 2024 RNC, July 13, 2024. The Amtrak Hiawatha is a train route that runs between Chicago and Milwaukee, offering frequent, reliable service with a focus on passenger comfort and convenience.

No 31 Amtrak Police Ford Expedition SUV K9, August 17, 2011.

The original Penn Station featured in the opening scene of the film "The Seven Year Itch" (1955); the film "The Clock" (1945) used interior shots of Penn Station and Stanley Kubrick's "Killer's Kiss" (1955) also filmed scenes in the passenger concourse of the original Penn Station.

No 32 Amtrak Police with K9 patrol Hiawatha two days before 2024 RNC July 13, 2024.

K9 units are primarily used for explosives detection and as a deterrent to crime in stations and on trains. These teams, composed of a dog and a handler, work to protect passengers, employees, and property by identifying potential threats.

No 33 Dodge Durango K9 SUV of the Amtrak Police in New York, July 22, 2011.

Amtrak has a significant number of K9 units, with some specializing in vapor wake detection, which allows them to detect explosives on moving individuals.

No 34 Passengers boarding and alighting the eastbound Lake Shore Limited at Buffalo–Depew station in September 30th 2016.

Amtrak Police prioritize the protection of the rail network and those who utilize it. This includes proactive measures like increased patrols on trains and along the Northeast Corridor and colaboration with other law enforcement.

No 35 Amtrak Police Ford Explorer Police Interceptor Utility, April 13, 2017.

Parked by a Tavern in the Square, South Station, Boston. South Station was first constructed in 1899 and soon became the busiest railroad station in America. Following a nationwide decline of railroad use, South Station experienced a deterioration in use, service and condition.

No 36 Amtrak Missouri River Runner train#313 pulling into Kirkwood Missouri Amtrak Station, July 2, 2010.

While the Missouri River and its surrounding areas have seen apprehensions related to other activities, such as drug smuggling, these incidents are not connected to the train service.

No 37 Amtrak Police Ford Explorer Police Interceptor Utility outside South Station, Boston, April 13, 2017.

South Station in Boston, a major transportation hub, has experienced some crime incidents, and around the Common near Tremont Street and Downtown Crossing there are areas of concern due to vagrancy, drug activity, and potential for altercations.

No 38 The Missouri River Runner (left) and eastbound Southwest Chief at Kansas City Union Station in May 2016.

This looks like a quiet place. A deadly shootout that occurred on June 17, 1933, known as the “Kansas City Massacre”.

No 39 Chevrolet Tahoe Amtrak Police K-9 Patrol vehicle with a Minnesota licence plate, October 5, 2012.

A bomb squad was called to Red Wing, Minnesota, after suspicious packages were found on an Amtrak train.

No 40 An Amtrak Shuttle laying over at Springfield Union Station in May 2013.

Police has been addressing issues of trespassing, disturbances, drug dealing, drug use and a shooting, which resulted in two arrests in and around the station.

No 41 Dodge Durango K9 SUV Seen near Penn Station, New York, October 22, 2024,

Midtown West, where Penn Station is located, is a vibrant area with attractions like Madison Square Garden, the Empire State Building, and Times Square.

No 42 Amtrak Keystone Service train 664 arrives at the Exton, Pennsylvania, USA station. Image includes main station building, high-level platform, train, and passengers waiting to board.

No 43 An Amtrak police Chevrolet Tahoe unit parked outside Union Station in Washington, DC, April 17, 2015.

Recent incidents, including a fatal shooting and an assault on a woman, have highlighted safety concerns at Washington D.C.'s Union Station. While some statistics show a decrease in crime near the station, high-profile incidents like these underscore the need for continued vigilance.

No 44 The first Miami-bound Floridian passing Roosevelt Road while departing Chicago in November 2024.

The Amtrak Floridian is a temporary, long-distance train route that provides a one-seat ride between Chicago and Miami. It combines the existing Capitol Limited and Silver Star routes to offer a direct service, avoiding a stop and train change in New York City.

Blueberry muffin on Amtrak's Cardinal

Photo by Sarah Stierch

Blueberry muffins are sold by many vendo but the Amtrak one is very satisfying and at a reasonable price.

Photo Crédits

No 1 Amtrak Police Officer in golf cart

https://commons.wikimedia.org/wiki/File:Amtrak_Police_Officer_in_golf_cart_in_front_of_Union_Station_at_50_Massachusetts_Avenue.jpg?uselang=eo

No 2 AMTRAK Police Officer at the Information Desk

https://commons.wikimedia.org/wiki/File:01.APD.PennStation.BaltimoreMD.25February2020_(49598850701).jpg?uselang=eo

No 3 Protecting America's railroads

https://commons.wikimedia.org/wiki/File:%22Protecting_America%27s_railroads%22_(7988169148).jpg?uselang=eo

No 4 An Amtrak Police SUV at the Lancaster Amtrak station

https://commons.wikimedia.org/wiki/File:Amtrak_Police_SUV_2.jpg?uselang=eo

No 5 Amtrak Police SUVs parked on 8th Avenue

https://commons.wikimedia.org/wiki/File:8th_Av_Penn_MSG_07_-_Amtrak_Police.jpg?uselang=eo

No 6 Amtrak Police K9 Unit at Union Station.

https://commons.wikimedia.org/wiki/File:01a.APD.UnionStation.WDC.31January2020_(49494083932).jpg?uselang=eo

No 7 A front view of Union Station, Portland, Oregon.

https://commons.wikimedia.org/wiki/File:A_front_view_of_Union_Station,_Portland_Oregon.jpg?uselang=eo

No 8 Amtrak Police SUV in front of the Washington D.C. station

https://commons.wikimedia.org/wiki/File:Amtrak_Police_SUV_Dog_Unit_Washington-400.JPG?uselang=eo

No 9 Amtrak Police June 7, 2016

https://commons.wikimedia.org/wiki/File:Amtrak_Police_(27207863013).jpg?uselang=eo

No 10 1st Annual POLICE K-9 MEMORIAL SERVICE CEREMONY

https://commons.wikimedia.org/wiki/File:1st_Annual_POLICE_K-9_MEMORIAL_SERVICE_CEREMONY_at_the_National_Law_Enforcement_Officers_Memorial_Central_Plaza_at_Judiciary_Square,_NW,_Washington_DC_on_Friday_afternoon,_11_May_2018.jpg?uselang=eo

No 11 Amtrak Police SUV

https://commons.wikimedia.org/wiki/File:Amtrak_Police_SUV_Washington_D.C.JPG?uselang=eo

No 12 Amtrak Police SUV

https://commons.wikimedia.org/wiki/File:Amtrak_Police_SUV_Dog_Unit_Washington.JPG?uselang=eo

No 13 Amtrak police, August 21, 2011.

https://commons.wikimedia.org/wiki/File:AMTRAK_Police_(6065793780).jpg?uselang=eo

No 14 AMTRAK Police Officer at Union Station.

https://commons.wikimedia.org/wiki/File:Amtrak_Police_IMG_7462_(50956631843).jpg?uselang=eo

No 15 The Amtrak Police Department is a railroad police agency

https://commons.wikimedia.org/wiki/File:Amtrak_Police_Chevy_Tahoe.jpg?uselang=eo

No 16 Amtrak police officer watches a special train at Burlington station in April 2015

https://commons.wikimedia.org/wiki/File:Amtrak_Police_SUV_Washington_D.C.JPG?uselang=eo

No 17 AMTRAK Police Department

https://commons.wikimedia.org/wiki/File:AMTRAK_Police_Department_(6055640991).jpg?uselang=eo

No 18 AMTRAK Police Officers at Union Station

https://commons.wikimedia.org/wiki/File:Amtrak_police_IMG_7467_(50957455587).jpg?uselang=eo

No 19 AMTRAK Police Department

https://commons.wikimedia.org/wiki/File:AMTRAK_Police_Department_(6056178288).jpg?uselang=eo

No 20 Amtrak Police SUV at Union Station

https://commons.wikimedia.org/wiki/File:Amtrak_Police_SUV,_Union_Station.JPG?uselang=eo

No 21 AMTRAK Police Department, August 17, 2011

https://commons.wikimedia.org/wiki/File:AMTRAK_Police_Department_(6056180380).jpg?uselang=eo

No 22 AMTRAK Police Officer at Union Station Lower Level

https://commons.wikimedia.org/wiki/File:AMTRAKPolice1.UnionStation.WDC.21January2017_(31851366903).jpg?uselang=eo

No 23 AMTRAK Police Department

https://commons.wikimedia.org/wiki/File:AMTRAK_Police_Department_(6056183078).jpg?uselang=eo

No 24 An Amtrak Police SUV

https://commons.wikimedia.org/wiki/File:Amtrak_Police_SUV.jpg?uselang=eo

No 25 AMTRAK Police Department

https://commons.wikimedia.org/wiki/File:AMTRAK_Police_Department_(6056185364).jpg?uselang=eo

No 26 Amtrak Police patrol Hiawatha

https://commons.wikimedia.org/wiki/File:Amtrak_Police_patrol_Hiawatha_two_days_before_2024_RNC_(Glenview_station)_IMG_37321.jpg?uselang=eo

No 27 AMTRAK Police Department

https://commons.wikimedia.org/wiki/File:AMTRAK_Police_Department_(6056189710).jpg?uselang=eo

No 28 The Stockton – San Joaquin Street Station

https://commons.wikimedia.org/wiki/File:Stockton_San_Joaquin_Street_Station_2319_15.JPG?uselang=eo

No 29 AMTRAK Police Department

https://commons.wikimedia.org/wiki/File:AMTRAK_Police_Department_(6057119807).jpg?uselang=eo

No 30 Amtrak Police patrol Hiawatha

https://commons.wikimedia.org/wiki/File:Amtrak_Police_patrol_Hiawatha_two_days_before_2024_RNC_(Milwaukee_Intermodal_Station)_IMG_3748.jpg?uselang=eo

No 31 AMTRAK Police Department

https://commons.wikimedia.org/wiki/File:AMTRAK_Police_Department_(6057665826).jpg?uselang=eo

No 32 Amtrak Police patrol Hiawatha

https://commons.wikimedia.org/wiki/File:Amtrak_Police_patrol_Hiawatha_two_days_before_2024_RNC_(Milwaukee_Intermodal_Station)_IMG_3753.jpg?uselang=eo

No 33 Dodge SUV of the Amtrak Police in New York

https://commons.wikimedia.org/wiki/File:Amtrak_Police_Dodge_New_York.JPG?uselang=eo

No 34 Passengers boarding and alighting the eastbound Lake Shore Limited

https://commons.wikimedia.org/wiki/File:Passengers_at_Buffalo%E2%80%93Depew_station,_September_2016.jpg?uselang=eo

No 35 Amtrak Police Ford Police Interceptor Utility

https://commons.wikimedia.org/wiki/File:Amtrak_Police_Ford_PIU_-2.jpg?uselang=eo

No 36 Amtrak Missouri River Runner

https://commons.wikimedia.org/wiki/File:AMTKtain313KWD.jpg?uselang=eo

No 37 Amtrak Police Ford Police Interceptor Utility

https://commons.wikimedia.org/wiki/File:Amtrak_Police_Ford_PIU.jpg?uselang=eo

No 38 The Missouri River Runner

https://commons.wikimedia.org/wiki/File:Two_trains_at_at_Kansas_City_Union_Station,_May_2016.jpg?uselang=eo

No 39 Chevrolet Tahoe AMTRAK Police K-9 Patrol vehicle

https://commons.wikimedia.org/wiki/File:Amtrak_Police_K9_Chevy_Tahoe.jpg?uselang=eo

No 40 An Amtrak Shuttle laying over at Springfield Union Station

https://commons.wikimedia.org/wiki/File:Amtrak_Shuttle_at_Springfield_Union_Station,_May_2013.JPG?uselang=eo

No 41 Seen near Penn Station

https://commons.wikimedia.org/wiki/File:Amtrak_Police_K9_Dodge_Durango.jpg?uselang=eo

No 42 Amtrak Keystone Service train 664

https://commons.wikimedia.org/wiki/File:Exton_station_as_Amtrak_Keystone_Service_train_664_arriving.jpg?uselang=eo

No 43 An Amtrak police unit parked outside Union Station

https://commons.wikimedia.org/wiki/File:Amtrak_Police_K9_Unit_Tahoe_(17192917256).jpg?uselang=eo

No 44 The first Miami-bound Floridian

https://commons.wikimedia.org/wiki/File:The_first_Floridian_departing_from_Chicago,_November_2024.jpg?uselang=eo

Special photos

https://commons.wikimedia.org/wiki/File:Blueberry_muffin_on_Amtrak%27s_Cardinal_-_June_2022_-_Sarah_Stierch_03.jpg?uselang=eo

https://commons.wikimedia.org/wiki/File:COOK_IN_THE_GALLEY_OF_THE_DINING_CAR_ON_AMTRAK%27S_SOUTHWEST_LIMITED,_CONSIDERED_BY_AMTRAK_AS_ONE_OF_THE_TOP_TWO_TRAINS..._-_NARA_-_555983.jpg?uselang=eo

https://commons.wikimedia.org/wiki/File:DINING_CAR_OFFERS_FRESH_FLOWERS_AND_GOOD_FOOD_ON_THE_SOUTHWEST_LIMITED,_AN_AMTRAK_TRAIN_BETWEEN_LOS_ANGELES..._-_NARA_-_555980.jpg?uselang=eo

https://commons.wikimedia.org/wiki/File:Amtrak_train_Capitol_Limited_30_-_dining_car_with_full-service_breakfast_3of3.jpg?uselang=eo

Chef on Amtrak´s Southwest Limited

Dining car offers fresh flowers and good food on the Soutwest Limited

Delicious breakfast served on Amtrak train Capitol Limited Train # 30 - dining car with full-service

About the author

Christian Berna loves Countryballs, trains, history and collects wooden trains.

The author thanks his parents for their support in creating this book.

Contact the author

missysclan@gmail.com
Published by www.missysclan.net

Cover:

Amtrak Police Ford Expedition K9 SUV by Tony Hisgett from Birmingham, UK June 7, 2016

https://commons.wikimedia.org/wiki/File:Amtrak_Police_(27207863013).jpg

Inside:

Gathering Before 1st Annual Police K-9 Memorial Service at the National Law Enforcement Officers Memorial Central Plaza at Judiciary Square (Detail)

https://commons.wikimedia.org/wiki/File:Gathering_Before_1st_Annual_POLICE_K-9_MEMORIAL_SERVICE_at_the_National_Law_Enforcement_Officers_Memorial_Central_Plaza_at_Judiciary_Square.jpg

More books by me:

- Palau in London
- U-Bahns
- The Adventures of USA and Poland
- American Heroes The Revolutionary War in Art
- Trains in Art
- Poland in Tibet
- The Story of Poland and USA
- Trains in Art 2

I would like to write more books in the future.

U-Bahns

ISBN 978-3-168-107-798

Christian Berna

2025

Palau in London

ISBN

Christian Berna

2025

The Adventures of USA and Poland

ISBN 9

Christian Berna

2025

American Heroes

The Revolutionary War in Art

US ISBN 978-3-313-646-349

Christian Berna

2025

The Story of Poland and USA

US ISBN

Christian Berna

2025

Poland in Tibet

US ISBN

Christian Berna

2025

Trains in Art

US ISBN

Christian Berna

2025

Trains in

Art 2

US ISBN

Christian Berna

2025

www.ingramcontent.com/pod-product-compliance
Ingram Content Group UK Ltd.
Pitfield, Milton Keynes, MK11 3LW, UK
UKHW040227290926
15471UKWH00001B/37

9 789713 246356